Fierce Fighters
SAMURAI

Charlotte Guillain

www.raintreepublishers.co.uk

Visit our website to find out more information about Raintree books.

To order:

☎ Phone 0845 6044371
🖷 Fax +44 (0) 1865 312263
🖳 Email myorders@raintreepublishers.co.uk

Customers from outside the UK please telephone +44 1865 312262

Edited by Rebecca Rissman, Nancy Dickmann, and Catherine Veitch
Designed by Joanna Hinton-Malivoire
Picture research by Tracy Cummins
Original iilllustrations © Capstone Global Library 2010
Original illustrations by Miracle Studios
Production by Victoria Fitzgerald
Originated by Capstone Global Library
Printed and bound in China by Leo Paper Products

ISBN 978 1 406 21614 1 (hardback)
14 13 12 11 10
10 9 8 7 6 5 4 3 2 1

ISBN 978 1 406 21713 1 (paperback)
15 14 13 12 11
10 9 8 7 6 5 4 3 2 1

British Library Cataloguing in Publication Data
Guillain, Charlotte.
Samurai. -- (Fierce fighters)
355.1'0952-dc22

Acknowledgements
The Bridgeman Art Library International p. **15** (© Look and Learn); akg-images p. **16**; Alamy pp. **17** (© Jon Bower London), **23** (© JTB Photo Communications, Inc), CORBIS pp. **21** (© Michael Maslan Historic Photographs), **22** (© Asian Art & Archaeology, Inc.); Getty Images pp. **7** (Erik Von Weber), **11** (Tohoku Color Agency), **19** (Felice Beato), **24** (ime & Life Pictures); Heinemann Raintree **pp. 28 top** (Karon Dubke), **28 bottom** (Karon Dubke), **29 top** (Karon Dubke), **29 bottom** (Karon Dubke); Photolibrary p. **10** (Radius Images); Shutterstock pp. **18** (© Anatoliy Samara), **26** (© Jose Gil); The Art Archive pp. **12** (Bibliothèque des Arts Décoratifs Paris / Gianni Dagli Orti), **14** (Bibliothèque des Arts Décoratifs Paris / Gianni Dagli Orti); THE Kobal Collection p. **27** (WARNER BROS. / JAMES, DAVID).

Front cover illustration of a samurai warrior reproduced with permission of Miracle Studios.

The publishers would like to thank Jane Penrose for her assistance in the preparation of this book.

Every effort has been made to contact copyright holders of material reproduced in this book. Any omissions will be rectified in subsequent printings if notice is given to the publishers.

Some words are shown in bold, **like this**. You can find out what they mean by looking in the glossary.

Contents

Two rulers are at war. Samurai run into battle to fight for their masters. These fierce **warriors** are afraid of nothing, not even death. Their weapons are deadly and their masks look like devils.

Surrender now or die fighting the samurai!

Samurai timeline

1500s	The samurai fight in many Japanese wars
1600s	Japan is peaceful
1800s	The samurai are banned in Japan
1900s	Japan fights in World War Two
2000s	You are reading this book

Who were the samurai?

The samurai were special **warriors** who lived in Japan. They were like knights. Rulers **hired**, or paid, samurai to fight in wars.

Where the Samurai lived

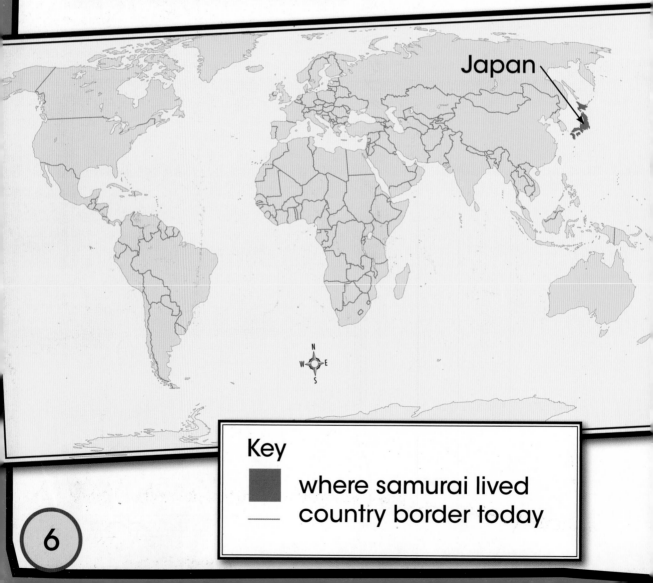

Japan

Key

where samurai lived
country border today

DID YOU KNOW?

Samurai means "those who serve".

Becoming a samurai

Only men from special families could be samurai. They started training when they were small children. They learned to fight with wooden swords. Later they learned to ride horses, shoot a bow and arrow, throw a **spear**, and fight.

The samurai had to learn how to use many different weapons.

DID YOU KNOW?

Samurai had to learn how to shoot a bow and arrow while they were riding a horse – not easy!

Samurai **warriors** learned **tactics**, or ways of fighting, that would help them win battles. But the most important samurai training was learning to use a curved sword with deadly skill.

Samurai practised many of the martial arts people still learn today.

DID YOU KNOW?

Young samurai also studied poetry and learned how to behave well.

Samurai rules

Most samurai **warriors** would only fight for one master. When his master was killed or **insulted**, a samurai had to find his master's enemy and kill him.

DID YOU KNOW?

Ronin were samurai who had no master. They would fight for anyone who paid them.

If a samurai **warrior** lost a battle then he would often kill himself. This was called *seppuku* (say *seh-poo-koo*). The samurai would take his sword and cut his own stomach open. He would rather die like this than be a **prisoner**.

DID YOU KNOW?

When a samurai did *seppuku* a friend would often cut his head off to finish the job quickly.

Samurai weapons

Samurai **warriors** wore a special suit of **armour**. Some samurai decorated their helmets with evil-looking masks to scare their enemies.

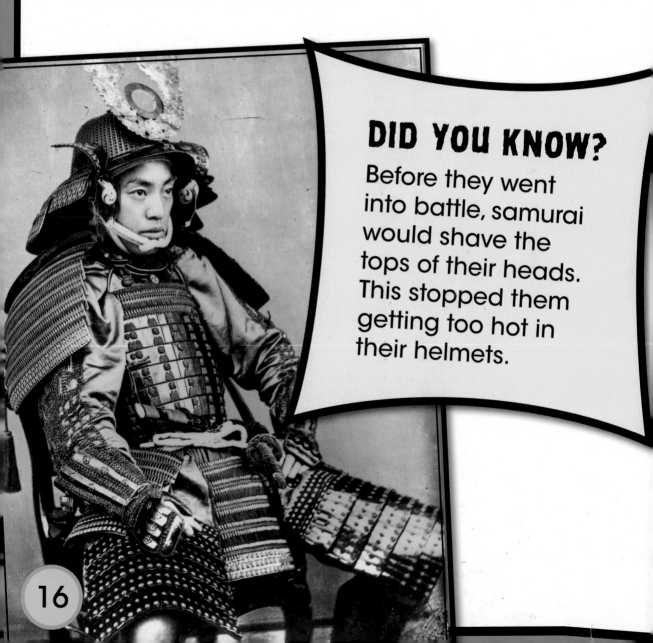

DID YOU KNOW?

Before they went into battle, samurai would shave the tops of their heads. This stopped them getting too hot in their helmets.

The most important weapon for a samurai **warrior** was his sword. Their curved swords were strong and had a sharp **blade**, or edge. They could cut a person in half with one slice. Samurai also had a shorter straight sword.

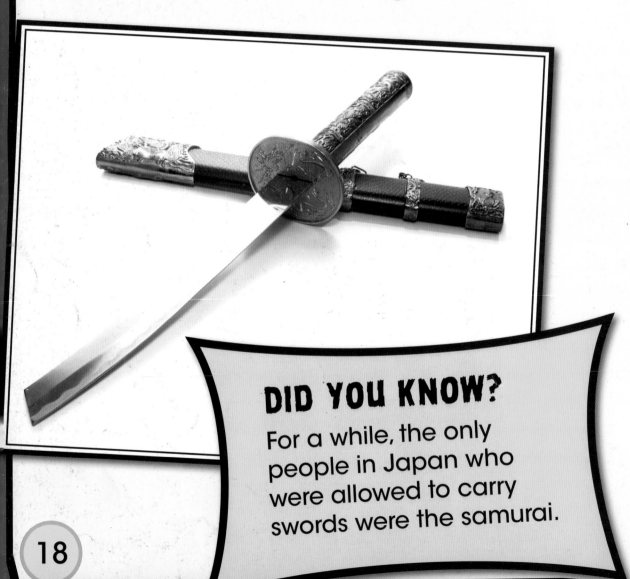

DID YOU KNOW?

For a while, the only people in Japan who were allowed to carry swords were the samurai.

19

Samurai **warriors** also used a *naginata*. This was a long pole with a sharp, curved **blade**. Women samurai liked to use this weapon. They spun the naginata to stop their enemies getting too close and then they stabbed them with the blade.

naginata

DID YOU KNOW?

When guns arrived in Japan, the samurai used them too. But they would always choose to use their swords first.

Famous samurai warriors

Sanada Yukimura was called the "number one **warrior** in Japan". But when he was beaten after a long battle he knew he must die. Sanada took off his helmet and the enemy cut off his head with one slice.

Sanada Yukimura

Uesugi Kenshin

DID YOU KNOW?

Some stories about the great warrior Uesugi Kenshin say he was killed by a samurai warrior as he used the toilet!

Samurai women

Samurai families taught young girls **martial arts**. Girls also learned how to use weapons. Women didn't usually fight in battle but they often had to keep their homes safe from attackers.

DID YOU KNOW?

One samurai story is about a woman **warrior** called Tomoe Gozen. She fought with her husband in many battles.

The end of the samurai

After many years people in Japan stopped fighting. One ruler took over and he **banned** samurai **warriors**. They were not allowed to wear their swords. Today the only samurai left are in films and cartoons.

DID YOU KNOW?

Many of today's **martial arts,** such as karate, kendo, and judo have changed very little since the samurai.

Samurai activity

Each samurai warrior had a personal flag, called a *sashimono*. He carried the flag on his back into battle.

Make your own sashimono

You will need:
- card
- small piece of cane
- string
- paints
- paint brushes
- scissors

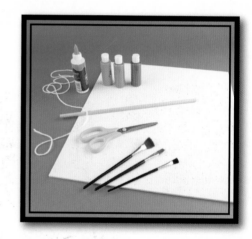

1. Cut out a card rectangle about 30cm × 40cm. Paint a design on the card. You could ask an adult to help you look up pictures of flags real samurai used.

2. When the paint is dry, make holes along one side of your flag. Use string to tie the flag to the piece of cane.

You are ready to march into battle!

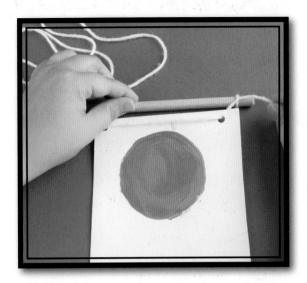

Glossary

armour covering made of metal or leather to protect a soldier

banned not allowed

blade flat, cutting part of a knife or sword

hire pay for a service or use

insulted say something rude about someone

martial arts traditional training of body and mind

prisoner person kept in a jail or prison

spear weapon with sharp point on a long pole

tactics way of doing something, such as fighting, to get results that are wanted

warrior fighter

Find out more

Books

Japan, Susan Crean (Wayland, 2010)

Japan: the Culture, Bobbie Kalman (Crabtree, 2008)

Samurai, Caroline Leavitt (Capstone Edge Books, 2007)

Places to visit

The British Museum, London
www.britishmuseum.org/

Visit the Japan Gallery at the British Museum to find out more about samurai.

Find out

Can you find out about Japan today?

Index